EMPTY NEST, SINGLE PARENT

Moving the Needle Toward a Repurposed Life

Carol Brzozowski

Dedicated to my sons Adam and Jonathan with love

CONTENTS

INTRODUCTION

"This could be our finest hour. To let go when we want to hold on requires utmost generosity and love. Only parents are capable of such painful greatness." - psychologist Dr. Haim Ginott

On a recent New Year's Eve, I cooked up a clam bake in my kitchen as the champagne chilled in the refrigerator.

I loaded up my outdoor fire pit with logs and lit a fire.

Joining me that night to usher in the New Year was my faithful companion: my dog.

My two sons – who as children would watch the ball drop on TV with me – were far away on this night, each engaged in their own holiday revelry in the cities in which they now lived a few hundred miles away.

Although I felt alone, I knew from statistics that there are millions of other single parents who also spend holidays alone as well as engage in other activities solo. For many of those years, the driving factor is custodial and visitation arrangements.

But when the children reach adulthood and leave the nest, the reason for single parent loneliness is this paradox: the custodial parent has done their job so well that the child has attained independence as is stated in the adage: 'We give them roots and we give them wings'. Because of that, the parent is likely to find herself physically alone.

While that New Year's Eve was no picnic for me despite the nice dinner I made myself and the cozy environment in which I partook of my holiday meal, it pales in comparison to some scenarios which I have witnessed where parents fearing that aloneness make it difficult for their children to leave home and attain their own independence.

'Empty nest syndrome', as it is called, describes a time of life when the last child leaves home. As difficult a transition it can be for the adult child, the parent experiences a unique kind of 'separation anxiety'.

According to the Mayo Clinic, while 'empty nest syndrome' is not a clinical diagnosis, it is a 'phenomenon' in which parents experience certain negative feelings when the last child leaves home.

Although the medical community does not regard it as a diagnosis, it often presents with many symptoms that under other circumstances might merit a visit to a mental health professional: depression, sadness, grief, loss of purpose, among many others.

Much of what has been written about the empty nest typically addresses it as being a time in life to reconnect with one's spouse. The challenges faced by a single parent empty nester are largely ignored.

The concept of the empty nest syndrome is a relatively new one in our history given three factors:

- Families used to be closer geographically, so it wasn't unusual to see adult children for Sunday dinner or other occasions. Now we are fortunate if we can see family members a few times a year.
- Our lifespan has increased, giving us many more years of life without child-rearing responsibilities. It begs the question: while we have more 'quantity' in our years, will we fill them with 'quality' of life?
- The divorce rate is higher than it was in the times in which many of us grew up, when women didn't have the economic power to leave marriages that did not serve them well.
- Some people have no choice, such as those people whose partners died before they were able to enjoy the fruits of their parenting labor together.

Thus, not only has the capacity for experiencing empty nest syndrome increased, but it hits the single parent that much more significantly. For the single parent empty nester, life has presented at least two major upheavals: divorce from or death of a spouse and the bittersweet day when the last child leaves the house.

A third layer is added when one becomes cognizant that this also is symbolic of another step in the aging process.

Your son or daughter has packed their bags and is off on their own journey, armed with the skills you've given them that augment their own natural talents and inclinations.

Meanwhile, you're left *unpacking* your bags, such as the baggage that may have accumulated through clinging to memories that are cluttering up the garage or attic or the emotional baggage from a relationship gone wrong with the adult child's other parent.

Perhaps in executing the myriad and endless tasks of child-rearing, you let your body, health and emotional well-being take second place to putting your family first.

Maybe you need to unpack that symbolic box into which you put your friendships, hobbies and passions.

Your financial fuel tank is possibly operating on fumes as in many states, child support ends at age 18 and you've been shouldering the greater part of the financial responsibilities for helping your children through college, trade school or another endeavor until they go off on their own.

Perhaps the thought of a romantic relationship was put on the back burner because you focused on your children and now the thought of getting into another relationship produces fear, anxiety, or resistance based on your previous experience with the children's other parent.

Your house – the walls of which may be sporting old crayon marks – is now ready not only for a fresh coat of paint, but an overhaul of repairs and repurposing the space.

I became a single parent when my sons were in elementary school. Financial issues were the driving factor leading me to file for divorce from my sons' father. After the divorce was final, I put my head down and rammed through their upbringing as best as I could, giving them every opportunity I could afford to on the income of a freelance journalist who was left to deal with financial devastation and also the consequences of the Great Recession.

I had to take pay cuts to keep my work with some clients while already living on less as a consequence of the divorce. Putting together enough jobs to meet my family's financial needs was a challenge with so many media companies shutting down during the Great Recession. I found myself competing with more people for fewer jobs.

My oldest son graduated from college and is employed in the profession of his choosing four hours away. He has bought a house. My youngest son is finishing an undergraduate degree and has wrapped up a year presiding over a fraternity. Both of my sons attained the Eagle Scout rank.

They've done just fine.

And so have I.

My goal in writing this book is to affirm the feelings of sadness, loss and grief of other single parents who are empty nesters. The feelings will subside and amplify as adult children go away and come back for visits and ultimately become more intense when they finally leave home to create their own life.

Single parents are known to pump significant amounts of time and resources into raising their children as they do not have another adult in the house whose needs they also must consider. The loss of identity and the sadness runs deep for single parent empty nesters.

This book also aims to offer hope: while this may be the end of one chapter in your life, there are plenty more pages to turn.

While I share my experiences of how I have met the challenges that single parent in the empty nest years have brought to me, it is up to you what you will be writing on those pages. I suggest that you get a journal and a pen or create a file on your computer and begin to draft a blueprint for the micro and macro changes you want to make in your life today that will establish a firm foundation for the next step in your journey.

CHAPTER ONE

SINGLE PARENTS

The pounding on my front door was abrupt and unanticipated.

I answered the door to find a uniformed police officer handing me an envelope. The contents informed me that my house was about to go into foreclosure.

Gripping the envelope with two shaking hands, I retreated to my bedroom, going past the hall where my two young sons were playing in their bedrooms. I closed the door, threw myself upon my bed and sobbed uncontrollably.

Another knock came, this time from one of my sons.

"Mama, what's wrong?"

What was wrong is that here I was – an educated, professional woman who had worked hard and saved a lot of money during my post-college single years – now facing the prospect that I would lose everything for which I worked through no fault of my own.

It is difficult for some people to grasp the concept that I did not regret marrying my sons' father because had I not met him, we would not have brought into this world two of the most amazing human beings.

I truly believe that most people try their best to keep a relationship intact, especially when it involves children. Nobody I know says to themselves when they are young: "I want to grow up, get married, get divorced and struggle."

In fact, I grew up playing on the front porch with my Barbie and Ken dolls. Barbie and I are the same age and so she set the stage for the cultural influences for girls my age who grew up thinking she was the role model for the way we were supposed to look and act and as such, some 'Ken' guy would take care of us.

The children in my neighborhood used to recite this little ditty about two people who appeared to like each other: "John and Jane (substitute any names here) sitting in a tree...K-I-S-S-I-N-G. First comes love, then comes marriage, then comes Jane pushing the baby carriage."

And they lived happily ever after.

Not quite.

As I tell my sons, a so-called 'broken home' has nothing to do with how many adults are under the roof raising the children. The broken home more aptly describes the relationship between the two parents and can often apply to parents living together under the same roof whose interactions make it difficult on everyone. They are living a lie "for the sake of the children" and children are smart enough to know the truth.

In my marriage, the problems were always financial in nature. Despite many attempts at therapy, it had reached a tipping point for me: I felt compelled to file for divorce. The financial stressors were there as part of the marriage and would be there after the divorce through battles over child support, but I felt that the divorce would at least stop the hemorrhaging.

After that first encounter with pre-foreclosure, which I stopped by cashing in most of my savings and investments I made before I got married, there would be two other times when my house would reach the brink of foreclosure. Each time, I was able to pull it back from the edge, always with the pro-bono help of one of two real estate attorney friends of mine.

Asking for help is critical for any single parent and I find that most of us are too proud to do so.

In the depths of my despair, I knew I was not alone. While the majority of children still live with both parents, the single parent scenario in the U.S. is quite prevalent. As the second decade of the 21st century draws to a close, some 23 percent of America's 74 million children live with a single mother.

That percentage has tripled between 1960 and 2016.

The financial implications are crushing.

A 2013 U.S. Census Bureau report on custodial mothers and fathers and their child support reveals that nearly 26 percent of custodial parents who were due child support had received no payments from noncustodial parents.

That's despite have an agreement for child support.

Child support ends in most states at the age of 18 unless other legal agreements are made to continue for other activities such as college, trade school, health insurance, or a disability.

Thus, providing for living expenses often becomes the sole responsibility of the parent with whom the young adult lives while home from college or until he or she becomes independent.

Many young adults, despite having come from a single-parent home, do phenomenally well once they get out on their own. They excel in their educational pursuits, in their occupations and enter into healthy relationships.

After the years of financial struggle to assure that their children have the best opportunities possible in life, single parents then finds themselves entering the empty nest phase on fumes.

This now becomes the time to fill the nest up again with that which supports you in your journey forward.

The empty nest phase invites the opportunity to design the next phase of your life. Start a journal in which you list goals for your physical and emotional well-being, your occupation, your family, your financial status, your spiritual health, your home, volunteerism and philanthropy, your social life (including friends and a significant other), your hobbies. This will serve as your blueprint, your mission statement and your compass in your journey forward.

CHAPTER TWO

EMPTY NEST

Two days after my 55th birthday and in the middle of my youngest son's senior year of high school, I took to my bed for my regular afternoon power nap.

At the sound of the three chimes that would always awake me following 27 minutes of napping, I started to rise from my bed. But the room started spinning violently. I felt paralyzed and totally out of control.

While I would come to find out that I had Benign Paroxysmal Positional Vertigo, the episode for me symbolized more: my life was spinning out of control. It was one of many manifestations that I would come to attribute to the new phase in life: 'empty nest syndrome'.

It's the great paradox of having achieved what you have worked for years to accomplish: teaching your child to be independent and then mourning the time when they actually do take the reins.

Oh, the irony! When our children are young, we are so eager to see them walk, hear them read, and marvel as they exhibit their growing independence.

Then comes the senior year in high school: the college application process, the prom (seeing them in 'grown-up' clothes), the high school graduation ceremony, the college campus tours, college orientation, college move-in day.... wait! Stop the clock!

No wonder it felt as if my life was spinning apart. The vertigo I had was followed by panic attacks during which I would feel 'trapped' inside of my car, in a restaurant or in any room. I was caught between feelings of being 'frozen' and wanting to bolt. What was happening to me?

Father's Day, 1981. I had loaded up my Ford Fairlane 500 with boxes packed full of my worldly possessions – including a newly-printed Bachelor's degree in journalism diploma from Central Michigan University – and headed to Florida for a job.

I hugged my mother and father goodbye, giddy with the anticipation of starting my first professional job as a newspaper reporter. I don't recall if my parents had cried that day, but during my subsequent yet infrequent visits, my father would always hint about a house that was for sale or a job that was available – it was his way of saying he missed me.

The phrase and practice of 'helicopter parenting' wasn't even a blip on the radar at that time. To be certain, it was rather common for many generations to live under the same roof as families ran farms and operated businesses together. Though my parents did not dissuade me, mine had been a bold move.

But was it really?

* * *

Only two generations ago, both sets of my paternal and maternal grandparents were boarding ships that carried them on a long journey from Poland and Czechoslovakia to the United States, leaving much of their family behind and in some cases, never to see many family members ever again.

As for me, I wanted to be a mother more than anything. I had tried for seven years to get pregnant with my firstborn. Figuring the stress of my job as a newspaper reporter was a driving factor in my inability to get pregnant, I left my job to become a freelance writer. Within months, I became pregnant.

I had raised my two sons as a single custodial parent since 2003 and even a few years prior to that when their father and I were separated off and on and there had been no legally mandated child support. As such, I had taken on more responsibilities than is typical in a two-parent family.

When I'd take my children out in public when they were young, people would say to me, "Enjoy this time with them. It goes by fast."

I filed that thought away, except for the sense of urgency which often underscored the tone of voice in which the message was delivered to me by those conveying it.

I had come to Florida alone. When my youngest son left for college, my life had come full circle – I was living alone in my house.

People would tell me, "You'll get used to it." But I didn't want to have a life to "get used to". I want a life to look forward to.

When I left my home in Michigan at age 21 to come to Florida, there was always something for me to look forward to: my first job, buying my first new car, getting married, buying a house, having children. As an empty nester, it had taken a concerted effort to create something to look forward to with anticipation.

It turns out that my roller coaster of feelings during my youngest son's senior year of high school were rather typical.

It's normal to feel as if the "letting go" experience is painful while at the same time a parent is actively encouraging a child to become independent, according to the Mayo Clinic. Difficult feelings arise with no children at home who need care and whose constant companionship and activities kept the days humming along.

Although they are out of sight, adult children are not out of mind and concerns over their safety and well-being can still gnaw at a parent's psyche.

As my sons each headed off to college, they would be facing a multitude of challenges: who would he become away from home? What did he want to do for a living? How would college help him achieve that? How would he approach relationships with the opposite sex? Where would he find a job? What family values would he retain and which ones would he shed to make room for his own beliefs? How would he handle eating habits, exercise and staying emotionally balanced? How would he develop the more rigorous study habits required in college? How would he navigate his social life – from roommates to classmates to the 'brothers' he would acquire when he joined a fraternity? What about time management? Money management?

The empty nest transition may be more difficult for those with an only child or those who strongly identified with their role as a parent (during a recent lunch date with a friend whose son is a junior in high school, I saw tears welling up in her eyes as she spoke of her only son getting ready for his college years).

How to handle such emotions can be critical for a successful separation as a profound sense of loss may lead to depression, alcoholism, identity crisis and marital conflicts, according to the Mayo Clinic.

In a journal, identify those factors that are tying you down to your past role and standing in the way of what you want for your life. Our life is lived in the present moment.

What will it take for you to honor the past, then let go of it and embrace the future your desire?

CHAPTER THREE

MY SONS, MY FRIENDS –
RELATIONSHIP REDEFINED

I remember the day my first-born started his first day of school like it was yesterday. It was a bittersweet moment: I had done everything I could to prepare him for this day, so I was confident he had the best shot at success that he could have.

Yet it also was a milestone day: a day I had to let go of his hand and pass him off to his teacher, who took his hand and guided him into her classroom. I bid him a tearful goodbye, and then stood in the courtyard "hiding" behind a post, watching him settle in until the bell rang.

I drove home, tears rolling down my cheeks.

A little more than a decade later, the bittersweet feelings returned when my son – who grew up to be much taller than me – was heading off for college at the University of Florida.

I was confident that I had done everything I could to prepare him for that day. I knew he would have the best shot at success that he could have at one of the best public universities in the country.

I helped him unload all of his personal items from our vehicle and bid him an emotional good-bye. It was a much longer drive back home. I would not see him again for a month until the family weekend that was hosted by the university. At that point, it was the longest I'd ever been separated from him.

My son had flown from the nest and onto his own path. From that point on, he'd call all of the shots for his own life.

It was a time that redefined our relationship.

When sending my youngest son to the University of Central Florida, the last seminar I attended at the parent orientation session was "Letting Go and Staying Connected" by Dr. Bill Blank, director of career development at the university's career services department.

I learned that the final year or so of high school can encompass months of emotional intensity that rival any two years of parenting as the child and parent struggle to let go and stay connected.

Parents of college-bound seniors may be engaged in helping their child in a number of tasks, including choosing and applying for colleges, figuring out the financing of the cost of college, exploring living options, attending orientations, and managing the change in their relationship.

Every 20 years, a new generation is defined by its societal events. Millennials are the most sheltered and protected generation in the history of the world, says Blank. Child-rearing has shed the "spare the rod, spoil the child" approach for a child-centered approach against the backdrop of the perception of an increasingly unsafe world from which a child needs to be protected, stemming from the launch of the 9/11 terrorist attacks on U.S. soil to social media creating more opportunities for 'bad people to do bad things' while on the other hand more easily drawing attention to those matters.

Contemporary technology such as cell phones with video chat capabilities facilitate more access between parents and students than in my college days when I shared the one telephone we had in our dorm hall.

According to Blank, the average time adult children and parents talk on the phone is six times a day, creating a situation in which they are more responsive to adult intervention.

Today's children get along better with their parents than those in previous generations, he adds.

On the other hand, the high expectations and pressures that millennial children face during their years at home from "over-involved" parents can spill over into their college years for young people who are in the post-adolescent and pre-adult stage.

When parents are overly-involved, a child feels more pressure to achieve parents' expectations, which in turn can create anxiety.

The separation process is a mutual one between parent and college student, says Blank. It is fraught with ambivalence in wanting life to remain the same, yet knowing change is necessary.

Woven into the process are emotional conflicts as a college student strives to function independently as an emerging adult while still maintaining emotional ties to parents and other family members. They need to have the opportunity to develop a campus support system.

There is the emergence of interdependence, as student and parent develop effective relationships with appropriate boundaries, says Blank. For parents, it involves developing a more adult relationship with their student and feeling comfortable with the role change, he adds.

A healthy student-parent relationship is important to overall college adjustment, including academic achievement and affective health, he says.

While new college students come to grips with the changes in their lives, so too do parents, says Blank.

Before college years, parents tend to set priorities and expectations for their children and their approach may be controlling, directing, telling, and prescriptive as they execute a role of provider and manager, he says.

The effective collegiate parent tends toward the student's passions and interests and takes on the role of facilitating, advising, listening, partnering, and coaching, Blank adds.

It's the evolution of life's roles: mother and father treat their offspring like children. Then comes a time when the relationship takes on a more adult-to-adult interaction. As mother and father age, there is the potential for their adult offspring to become the caretaker of an ailing, aged parent.

One of the benefits of the new dynamics a parent cultivates with a college student is that of the adult-to-adult relationship. I love it when my older son cooks me dinner or helps me troubleshoot my computer problems. I love it when my younger son advises me on new trends or offers a listening ear when I have a concern.

In the new dynamic, the parent is not always the leader of the adult children but is open to be taught by them and walk as equals in the world.

Notes Blank: "Isn't it wonderful to let go of some of that pressure?"

Many parents have to grieve the old relationship before they are ready to accept the new one, Blank says.

Something else he says hits home: "Flow with transitions in a way that does not cause feelings of guilt or abandonment."

I came to appreciate the emotions that I demonstrated and how I reacted to the events that unfolded during my son's senior year of high school and start of college would affect how he would be able to cope.

If doing parenting 'right' was a priority to me all of these years, then why drop the ball now, I reasoned? What good would it do my son to see me falling apart because he was leaving?

What messages was I sending him? That I feared he couldn't handle his independence? That he needed to worry about his mother back home becoming emotionally unraveled? That one cannot enjoy life at every stage and one's potential for happiness stops when the children leave home? Would this be what he, too, would have to look forward to should he reach this stage?

During my oldest son's college orientation, which the University of Florida calls "Preview", I attended a seminar called "Family Transitions", moderated by the university's Counseling and Wellness center.

I affectionately referred to it as 'group therapy' for parents sending their first-born off to college. Even looking at the seminar's title on the program triggered tears.

Recently, a young man at the gym where I worked out indicated to me that as a new college student, he was both excited and nervous. While as parents we may focus on our own emotions at this time, it also is an emotionally turbulent time for our sons or daughters, as well as siblings and even the family pet.

In the college student's first days, he or she may experience a roller coaster of emotions.

There are issues associated with leaving home, such as displacement of traditional support systems, knowledge of a familiar environment, change in friendships and changes in familiar expectations.

There's uncertainty about the future. A student's goals may be idealized and untested in the new environment.

Although students are aware that study demands in college are different, many are unprepared for the amount of and rate at which the material will be presented. While many have been successful in high school, receiving an average grade may come as a shock. It takes time to see the bigger picture and the learning process over a semester.

What the student thinks others expect of him or her is very important. Living up to or failing those goals can be a source of motivation and reward but also stress and shame.

There's the "hidden curriculum" of college: how does one navigate the campus, pay bills, balance a checkbook, shop for groceries, find classrooms, ensure they're in the right course, be on track for their major, approach a professor, ask for help with academics, figure out where to eat, do laundry, manage differences with roommates, and the myriad of tasks that were once taken for granted or provided by others? Can anyone help? Is it even OK to ask for help?

Fitting in socially also is a significant concern: developing friendships, intimacy and social support is desired but takes time. Where does one go to initiate these important aspects of community life? How does one cope with difficulties in creating a social network?

For some students, making independent decisions can be daunting. How does a student decide how to act and what options to choose? Who will approve or disapprove of those options?

So what can parents do to help make the transition to college go as smoothly as possible for their offspring? The center's counseling staff acknowledged there are no easy answers for parents and family members. There are some general guidelines:

- Listen to your student's concerns; avoid lecturing or too quickly offering solutions.
- Ask questions to help your student clarify the concerns; avoid giving answers too readily.
- Acknowledge and communicate emotions – affirming that you recognize your student's feelings and avoid denying the presence of strong feelings (in yourself or your student).
- Express your thoughts and provide perspective; avoid making demands.
- Help clarify the consequences of behaviors; avoid threatening in ways that stifle communications.
- Be supportive and remind them you love them; avoid taking responsibility away from your student.
- Strive for mutual respect; avoid demanding submission without understanding.
- Let go a little and compromise where possible; avoid giving up completely.
- Deal with the problems openly and as calmly as possible; avoid ignoring or exaggerating problems.
- Allow mistakes for both of you; avoid expecting perfection...growth takes time.

To be sure, starting college is a highly emotional time for students and their families. The tension can be high. Counselors have seen a range of scenarios, from those parents who've had a strained relationship with their students and drop them off at college and spin off in their cars to those who book a hotel for a week and keep checking on the student on a frequent basis.

Siblings may either feel sad or are none too happy to try to take over their brother or sister's room (this is not the time to re-purpose the room, however).

The University of Florida's Dean of Students' office offered us parents several other suggestions for families to help support their student.

A helicopter parents hovers; a rocket ship parent takes issues straight to the top. Avoid those behaviors, but do be involved and stay informed. Be aware of deadlines, resources and opportunities.

Encourage your student to get involved in at least one extracurricular activity; these help ensure a successful transition. That activity can be connected with the student's academic or social interest or can enhance an activity in which she or he is interested.

Encourage your student to do research with a professor or study abroad.

Discuss expectations about substance abuse, money management, wellness and integrity.

Communicate frequently, but ask your student what he or she prefers: phone calls, texts, video chats or Facebook. Don't make surprise visits to the campus; ask the student if the time is convenient, as they may need study time.

Trust your instincts – if you are concerned for your student's well-being, contact the dean of students.

The best advice to give your student: everything at the university is a learning experience – including that which happens outside the classroom.

That's also a concept worth embracing for the student's family members as well.

As one of your last acts as parenting a human being who is letting go of your hand and embarking on their own path, ponder ways in which you can model for your adult child how they can successfully navigate life's transitions. Your son or daughter is going through the stresses associated with crossing the bridge from dependence to independence and it can be frightening to them to see a parent having problems. To the extent that you can, avoid burdening them with your own challenges by discussing them with friends, family members or a professional. On the other hand, enjoy the transition of your relationship with your son or daughter from parent-child to adult-adult, such as having them cook you a meal or drive you to a place where you both enjoy hanging out.

CHAPTER FOUR

LACK AND WEALTH

By far, for me, the most difficult part of the single parenting journey has been the financial piece. The break-up of my marriage was rooted in financial causes and while the divorce stopped the bleeding, the wound continued to fester.

In many states, child support stops at age 18 unless a legal agreement for other expenses such as college or health insurance stipulate otherwise. After both of my sons turned 18, I paid for all of their expenses that they could not otherwise finance through college scholarships, grants, loans and income from their own jobs.

I continued to pay for their health insurance, dental insurance, some phone expenses, furnishing their dorms and their living expenses when they were home on break.

Whether an empty nest single parent has a job outside of the home or is self-employed as I am, these years can be more of a financial challenge than the child-rearing years. Marriage to someone else can penalize the family, as school loans are predicated on household income and unless the other partner has the means or will to finance your college student's education, the student financially suffers for it. If they have their own children, it is unlikely they will help share the financial costs of college for your children. I always told my sons one of the greatest gifts I gave them was to stay single as it made them eligible for more loans.

Being a single parent also raises a number of issues when dating and in deciding who pays for what. In a post-divorce relationship of 12 years, my partner at that time had significantly more money than I did. He also had a family whose members may have frowned upon any significant help he may have given me. And yet, being self-employed, any time I took off to be with him meant I was losing income-generating time.

Being in that situation was like being a hamster in a wheel. While he would float money to help me with bills, the bottom line was I didn't have the means to pay him back or else I wouldn't have asked for his help in this first place.

With the disruption of so many industries, I suspect that these are hard times for a lot of people and crushing for those who are empty nester single parents. I am proud to say I made it through the recession and through a media bloodbath – as a journalist, the number of jobs began to shrink as media outlets consolidated or folded. I have managed to rebuild credit that circumstances external to me had destroyed.

As a self-employed person, revenues don't come by way of consistent weekly or bi-weekly paychecks that those who work on a staff receive. Yet I have friends in jobs who cannot say with certainty they will still be in that job within a year.

It's rather amusing to hear financial planners talk of how to save for a comfortable retirement – and perhaps two-parent families are able to put aside money for their retirement years – but many empty nest single parents are just scraping to get by.

These days, many of us live far away from family members who might be able to provide help and in transient communities in which people move in and out. Under these circumstances, it is difficult to establish a financial support system.

And just as we are financially helping our sons and daughters cross the educational finish line before they launch their own careers, our own retirement starts to come into focus and for many of us, that prospect can be daunting from a financial point of view.

Certainly, there are small measures an empty nest single parent can take to help secure his or her own financial future: paying off a mortgage, cutting the TV cable cord to replace it with digital services, taking advantages of AARP discounts (for which you can qualify at the age of 50), taking a brutal look at your expenses and budget and make the necessary adjustments.

Consider that while some of your friends in intact relationships may be retiring while you may have to work more years beyond the traditional retirement age.

It's a matter of shifting your priorities to that of providing for your family to making the changes needed to provide for your retirement.

This also can be a time to reinvent your career. Perhaps it's time to enter the gig economy and derive your income from several sources. This may be the opportunity to go back to school and get a degree in something you've always wanted to pursue, but never had the time to do so. Try volunteering somewhere – perhaps it will lead to a paid position.

As single parents, we are unable to financially provide everything we wanted for our children. As such, many of our children had to work when they became of age to do so.

But the wealth lies in this: our children learned the value of work and how work leads to independence and the ability to provide for one's own needs and wants. As many children of single parents become adults, the transition to independence becomes easier as they had already by that time learned to do for themselves what parents had done for their children in other households.

A friend of mine once told me the greatest gift you could give a child is to teach them to be able to manage on their own. If something were to happen to you, they would be able to carry on without feeling helpless because they know what they need to do.

There are only three ways to make it through the financial challenges of empty nest single parenting: make as much money as you can, save as much money as you can and live within your means. When you feel down about your situation and feel a bit remorseful that you weren't able to give your children everything that other children had, remember the values that your children will inherit, including independence.

CHAPTER FIVE

NEST REPURPOSED

Oprah Winfrey speaks of having a home that "rises up to meet you". What she means is creating a space that nurtures and affirms you. A space where you want to reside, not a space from which you want to escape.

My house suffered through the divorce and its aftermath. What money I had first went to the care of my sons. There was nothing left for home improvements after the struggle to keep the roof over our heads and the lights on. I had qualified for a new roof through a county financial assistance program at no cost to me as long as I stayed in my house for 10 years. I wasn't going anywhere anytime soon, so the new roof went up on my house.

But once my sons turned 18 and the child support stopped, even more of my income was going to the care of my sons through their college years. With them not being in the house, any financial assistance for home improvements were out of my reach as my income was considered too much to qualify but was not enough to keep up with all of the demands of an old house.

Because we live in a time when the Great Recession of 2008 kicked most of us hard in the gut, I had to take pay cuts to keep some of my clients in freelance writing, I appreciate the fact that I do have a roof over my head. It has taken many years for people to recuperate from that. Think of how it has impacted single parents.

The decision to stay in a house or leave it after your children leave the nest is predicated upon many factors. While a newer house – even if it is a 'downsized' version of a family home – may come with warranties on roofs, appliances and other mechanical features, its mortgage may be higher than that of the older house, for which the mortgage is smaller and gets lower with each month's payments. Financial concerns on older homes focus more on repairs.

The option of renting places one at the mercy of the landlord's whims of raising the rent as he or she sees fit.

My decision has been to stay, pay down the mortgage and take on the repairs one by one. With my youngest son still in college, it's still important for me that he has a 'home' to come to with his room still intact until such a time he is out on his own.

With that a given, de-junking what is in the house has been my focus.

De-junking after your sons or daughters leave the house is initially a difficult task. Many items are imbued with memories and it's difficult to pare it down. Most single parents during the child-rearing years do not have time to de-junk let alone time to execute the day-to-day tasks of child-rearing and housekeeping on top of job demands.

So not only is there emotion involved in de-junking, but volumes of it. While it might almost look like hoarding, for me, it's emotions I've hoarded more than material items.

I would address the mess in the garage and around the rest of the house in short spurts until one day, I started to see the light at the end of the tunnel. My house was more orderly. It freed up time for me to start the next task at hand.

The process was long and arduous. If it meant giving myself the space to sit with an item and cry over it (either happy tears over good times with my sons or grief over the loss of a marriage), I gave myself permission to go through the emotions.

Then I'd either throw it out, put it in a box for donations or if I felt I needed to keep it, I put it in a place designated for that item. Many times, I put items out to the curb on garbage pick-up day because one person's trash can be another person's treasure. I was glad to see it would be of value to someone else and not end up in precious landfill space.

It's taken several years to get to this point. Mindfulness meditation has done wonders in helping me over this hurdle. I had to make peace with the fact that while the circumstances in which I found myself and had to raise my sons in originated with external factors such as the divorce and the Great Recession, that it would be me and only me leading myself out of the consequences – no one else was going to do it for me.

I turned my thinking around to appreciating all I had and that it was my own efforts – with some help from my sons – that are the driving forces behind what I have today.

It gave me an appreciation that while the house in which I live in isn't the best-looking in town, it is mine. I worked hard to keep this house. Instead of resenting it, I have gratitude for it – the roof over my head, a chair on a patio on which to sit and listen to the birds sing, the wave of neighbors as I walk my dog.

Pushing through this very difficult task of de-junking and doing so with success opened up more time for me to put into activities I enjoy more.

Another challenge of living alone after my sons left was the fact that I was eating alone. It hit me when I went grocery shopping for the first time after my youngest child left home for college: I was buying for one and cooking for one.

Initially, I would order out a lot and take the food home or just slap something together to eat and consume it while watching TV. While that's OK on some occasions, it came to symbolize to me that I was not regarding myself as being as important as my family members or company for whom I'd make nice meals and set them out at the dinner table.

When my sons come back to visit, I endeavor to make them their favorite meals. I try to make extra food for them to take back in a cooler. I always promulgate food traditions for holidays. So why would I not treat myself the same way I treat others when it comes to food preparation and the environment in which I consume it?

I soon redefined my meal preparations and where I took my meals. I began to make meals that were nourishing and creative. I pulled out recipes for favorite dishes. Naturally, there would be leftovers, which would make a delicious lunch the next day. Or I'd freeze them for another meal on a night when I didn't have time to cook because I was gradually re-inventing a life that didn't center just on work and sleep.

I started taking my meals at the kitchen table again instead of in front of the TV set. I light candles. I also take meals out on my patio, enjoying the sounds of my neighborhood. Eating out can be expensive, but I will do so on occasion with friends.

The house is quiet without my sons. On the other hand, I play the music I want as loud as I want. I order the day as I want. To do so isn't coming from a place of happiness that they're gone (I've met parents for whom child-rearing was not pleasant and they felt nothing but relief for their children's departure). I love having my sons visit. I cry when they leave. Playing my music loud and going about the house as I choose is a way of giving myself permission to carry on...with gratitude for what I've accomplished for them and for myself.

Little by little, I am creating a space that now centers on me, yet still invites my sons – and others – to visit.

Give yourself credit for creating a home in which your child was able to thrive. Start de-cluttering your home, earmarking items to keep, donate, sell, or discard. Consider a minimalist lifestyle in which you pare down to only what you need and truly desire, creating space for an environment that nurtures you. Those mementos of the past that you choose to not let go can be stored away.

CHAPTER SIX

GET OUT!

Soon after my youngest son moved out to go to college and I began to enter my empty nest years, I was at a hair appointment when my hair stylist advised me that the best action I could take on my own behalf was to accept every invitation I got.

A significant part of the life of a single mother is focused on the children, especially in an effort to do the job at times of two parents. The adult child's exit from the home takes what was once a life of sprinting through the day to a virtual crawl.

Being self-employed and working from home means I'm somewhat socially isolated anyway. Add to that living alone after my sons left home for college and work and the social isolation increases...especially given the fact that they – my nearest kin – are nearly 200 miles away.

It has meant that every holiday for which I used to spearhead the celebration for a family is now spent alone unless I make other arrangements beforehand.

There's a song we used to sing in Girl Scouts: "Make new friends but keep the old...one is silver and the other gold."

Before you had children, your social life most likely focused on childhood friends, college buddies and work associates. When you become a parent, some – if not all – of those friendships are put on the backburner while new ones emerge in the creation of a support group of other parents.

When the children leave home, some of the parental friendships may fall by the wayside as issues such as carpooling and school fundraising are no longer part of one's daily responsibilities and so you may spend less time connecting with other parents.

One day, you're eating with other parents at the spaghetti dinner fundraiser and then before you know it, you're eating alone in front of the TV.

And so when I can, I do accept every invitation I possibly can. There's an old saying: 'One thing leads to another.'

You never know where an invitation might take you: to a new job, a new friend, a new partner, a new hobby. As you expand your social circle, you are expanding your support system as well.

From the time I became an empty nester, I accepted a number of invitations that led to new friends and opportunities.

Take care, though, that the people with whom you surround yourself with are lifting you up and energizing your spirit. As you move through the emotions of dealing with the empty nest transition, you need fuel to move forward – not negatively to drag you down.

I became active in swimming after taking up on an invitation to join the U.S. Masters Swimming group in my city. Accepting that invitation led to meeting new friends and attending social events. It led to meeting one friend in particular who was an immigrant from Venezuela and who helped me clean up my property in the aftermath of a hurricane. It led to me becoming more healthy and fit.

Accepting an invitation to join with a group of young black professionals to watching the U.S. presidential debates led me to meeting new friends. It led me to one young friend in particular who gave me a ride to Miami so we could watch a vice presidential candidate make a campaign stop. It led me to lend my support for a young man running for a city commission seat and getting more involved in city politics.

Accepting an invitation to serve on a citizen's committee in my city has led me to meet everyone from the vice mayor to the police chief to code compliance officers, all of whom are there to assist when I need something.

Getting out to the dog park led me to meet friends who took me out on my birthday when I was alone that day. Going to beach yoga by myself on New Year's Day led me to meet a few other women who invited me to dinner with them.

Going to a candlelight vigil for the victims of a mass shooting led me to meet a woman whose empathy has been a bedrock of support whenever I need a good cry.

Accepting an invitation to my high school class reunion and the offer of an airplane ticket from a friend of mine led me to meet my boyfriend.

Everywhere I go, I take my business cards in an effort to network with people, not just professionally, but personally.

One of my single mother friends drove Route 66 from east to west – all by herself. Another drives from Florida to Pennsylvania to visit family, with her only driving companion being her dog. One friend flew to Australia by herself to be with her children. Another flew alone to India.

In many cases one thing has indeed led to another....and another.

Going to functions alone is not necessarily easy or enjoyable but go anyway. Invitations will take you to new places where you will meet new people and expand your horizons beyond the box in which we sometimes place ourselves as empty nest single parents. Make it a point to strike up a conversation with at least one new person every time you get out.

CHAPTER SEVEN

MIND, BODY AND SOUL

While parents are awash in their own emotions over the empty nest, their sons or daughters may have other concerns about their parents. Adult children of divorce worry about the health or financial welfare of both parents whereas with those who come from intact families, that concern is not so pronounced as both parents presumably are taking care of each other in their older years.

I never want my sons to worry about having to take care of me to the extent that I have control over that situation. The empty nest years are a time to take stock of one's own physical well-being. The physical, emotional and social benefits of exercise are well-documented.

The child-rearing years can often leave little time for taking care of one's own physical health in terms of exercise. Many of us pack on weight and as we enter middle age, it becomes more challenging to get back to a healthy weight.

As my sons headed off to college, I eventually developed a fitness routine that included swimming three times a week at 6 a.m. with a U.S. Masters Swimming group. I also do weight-bearing exercise in the gym. I've augmented the routine with various forms of yoga, both in the studio and on the beach.

Choose a form of exercise you enjoy to ensure your commitment. While you are exercising, you also are socializing.

* * *

Swimming has helped me lose weight and firm up more than any other form of exercise. It also is easy on the joints and is not prone to injury, as are other forms of exercise. I encourage people to swim, but many people who see the Masters Swimming group in the morning are reticent, thinking that they have to be competitive. You be what you want: go for the fitness only or work to compete and a coach is on hand to help you with your form and give you work-outs.

Masters basically means you're of adult age and swimming is something you can do at any age.

According to U.S. Masters Swimming, swimming is an 'all in one' exercise that provides a multitude of benefits.

Among its physical benefits swimming lowers blood pressure, reduces bad cholesterol and increases good cholesterol, helps weight loss and weight maintenance, is easy on joints, improves the immune system, preserves and improves functional capacity, strengthens muscles through the resistance of water, and improves flexibility.

Swimming's additional benefits include slowing down the aging process, reducing risk for heart disease and diabetes, reducing chronic pain, improving muscle imbalances, developing lung capacity, exercising nearly every muscle in the body, lowering cortisol, and improving sleep.

There are mental benefits as well. Swimming enhances the connections between left and right brain hemispheres, prevents brain shrinkage, can help produce new brain cells, improves problem-solving skills and memory, reduces stress, allows you to 'disconnect' from outside stimulation, reduces depression and anxiety.

Other mental benefits of swimming include improved self-control and willpower, relaxation from the repetitive nature of movement, improved self-esteem and mental toughness.

In Master's swimming, a coach will help you with your goals. Aside from a swim suit, you can get as much gear as you want.

Goggles are necessary to protect your eyes from the chlorinated water. Ear plugs help keep water out of your ears. After you swim, a drop or two of rubbing alcohol in your ear helps dry them out.

A swim cap keeps hair out of the pool and under control so it's not flopping around in your face. You can go online to find shampoo especially formulated for swimmers' hair.

Fins for swimmers are different than fins for diving or snorkeling.

A paddle is used to hold onto as you propel yourself through the water while using fins (or not). Hand paddles, which you tether to your hands, are used to help build upper body strength.

A pull buoy is placed between your legs and helps rotate your body so you can work on form.

A snorkel (not the type used in snorkeling or diving) is used to work on breathing exercises.

You can store everything in a mesh sports bag, ideal for the wet swimming items to drain and dry off. A dry bag separates the dry items from the wet ones.

You may not think you are sweating when you are exercising in water, but you are and you need to hydrate yourself, so it's good to have a water bottle.

* * *

Yoga is an ancient practice for which its benefits are well documented. The American Osteopathic Association credits yoga -- which combines postures, meditation and breathing – for its physical and mental benefits.

Physical benefits include increased flexibility, muscle strength and tone; improved respiration, energy and vitality; maintaining a balanced metabolism; weight reduction; cardio and circulatory health, improved athletic performance and protection from injury.

Its mental benefits include the ability to manage stress better with relaxation techniques, experience less chronic pain, lower blood pressure, and reduce insomnia. Increased concentration and more focused attention are other mental benefits.

There are many different types of yoga, so it's best to try sample classes at various studios to ascertain what is a good fit for you.

Yoga helps me to stretch, strengthen my balance and quiet the mind. People I know are afraid of yoga because they think they need to stand on their heads or twist into a pretzel shape.

While some people can do that, a good yoga instructor helps you with poses and encourages you to go only as far as your body wants to take you without pain.

Sometimes that involves props that move beyond the simple yoga mat.

A bolster is used under various parts of the body to provide support for poses. Blocks can help you in postures where you need assistance to elevate a certain body part to get into and stay into a posture.

A belt is used to help extend your legs or arms further.

A bag that is filled with rice or sand is sometimes used on your belly for breathing. A Mexican blanket can be used as a mat, a prop for support or to cover yourself in meditative yoga.

You can find yoga clothes at a lot of places now. Wear something that offers comfort and flexibility. I like yoga pants for cooler weather and favor the harem-style pants for warm weather, as they breathe nicely.

* * *

In addition to swimming and yoga, I go to the gym twice a week for targeted upper body and abs/legs weight-bearing exercises. This is essential for building muscle to strengthen the bones and stave off osteoporosis. Essential for the gym is to get a workout designed for you by a certified personal trainer. He or she will show you proper form to avoid injuries and give you a workout to help build muscles and firm up. Plans need to be switched up occasionally to challenge your muscle groups.

* * *

Hand-in-hand with an exercise routine is good eating habits. There are dozens of diet plans on the market and many of them seem to be trendy. What is good for you is going to depend on what your body needs. The important factor is to not use food as an emotional crutch during the empty nest years. It's far too easy for us to grab something to eat at a drive-through and eat in front of the television set.

Instead, opt for cooking yourself healthy meals because you deserve it just as much as each member of your family did when they sat at the dinner table in your home.

* * *

One of the best habits to start establishing for yourself is that of mindfulness or meditation. Single empty nesters are no different than anyone else in that we can obsess about the past and worry about the future but have difficulty zoning in on living in the present moment, thus missing the life that's happening right in front of us.

More than 20 years ago, Jon Kabat-Zinn at the University of Massachusetts Medical School developed Mindfulness-Based Stress Reduction (MBSR), a program focused on using meditation and breathing techniques.

Research on the technique has shown to have therapeutic benefits for those experiencing stress, anxiety, high blood pressure, depression, chronic pain, migraines, heart conditions, diabetes and other ailments, notes Dave Potter, a fully-certified MBSR instructor, adding that participants also report feeling more "alive" and "in tune" with themselves.

There also are good apps that offer guided meditation, such as Calm, Insight Timer and Headspace, among others.

Another way of honoring your mind is to endeavor to learn something new. Why should your son or daughter be the only one to expand their minds through education? The beauty of being older is that you can take a class just for the sake of learning instead of earning a degree. Check out classes at your local college that are open for you to do so and learn something new. Perhaps you really do want to earn a degree in the subject matter of your choosing.

Or learn a new language with the goal of traveling to a foreign land.

Choose a form of exercise you enjoy and commit yourself to it as to derive the physical, mental and social benefits it offers you in your empty nest years. Plan menus for the week as to ensure you are consuming healthy food; freezing leftovers helps to save money and time. Invite a friend over for dinner or to have a meal out to minimize the uncomfortable feelings that can emerge from eating alone. Incorporate meditation as a daily practice. Starting with just three minutes, setting a timer and focusing on your breath is a great way to clear your head and set the stage for the remainder of the day.

CHAPTER EIGHT

FOR THE LOVE OF DOG AND OTHER ANIMAL COMPANIONS

When my sons were growing up, they wanted a dog. I had rejected the idea because I didn't have surplus money – or the time – to take care of another living being. We didn't have a fenced-in yard.

I didn't grow up with a dog, so I didn't have a point of reference for what it was like to take care of them.

I grew to love dogs through the first relationship I had following my divorce in which my partner had a dog. After that relationship ended, I was pretty confident that I could care for a dog. Since I work from home, the dog and I would have a symbiotic relationship in that I would always be there for the dog and the dog would always be there for me.

You can't beat the feeling of being greeted at the front door by a dog wagging its tail, acting like you are the most important being on the planet every time you enter your home. Or a purring cat in your lap.

Soon after my youngest son went off to college and my post-divorce long-term relationship ended, I was ready to get my own dog. I not only wanted a dog for companionship, but it also tapped into the nurturing part of me that raised my sons, a feeling that receded in the background as my sons increasingly learned to take care of themselves.

I also wanted a dog for personal safety.

I started to scroll the website for the Humane Society of Broward County, looking at the photos of dogs up for adoption. I had identified three Labrador Retrievers that were of interest.

One day when both of my sons were home on a visit, we went to the Humane Society so I could meet the three dogs. While we were meandering through the shelter looking at the animals, my oldest son was crouched on the floor making a connection with one particular puppy. The sign indicted she was a 'Lab mix'.

She was interacting with my oldest son in such a way that she scored a spot on the list of dogs with whom we wanted to visit to see which one would be the best fit.

My sons and I sat in a waiting room as the shelter volunteers would bring each of the dogs to us. One dog didn't like men. Another had physical problems that were beyond my ability to financially address. A third seemed nonchalant.

But when the dog that connected with my older son came into the room, she bounded about, jumping into each of my sons' laps and kissing them, then coming over to me and doing the same. She looked out of the window at the other dogs that were playing outside.

"I'll take this one," I said.

We named her Leia.

I literally rescued Leia that day because as it turned out, there wasn't any Labrador Retriever in her. DNA tests revealed she was an American Staffordshire Terrier and Chinese Shar-Pei mix. So, she was part pit bull and as such, faces discrimination in many communities.

We'd be the perfect pair: this misunderstood pit bull and this marginalized single parent. She is both protective and loving. No one wants to mess with me when I walk about with this pit bull. She barks at anyone who comes near the house. She barks at the garbage collection vehicle. But behind closed doors, she cuddles up in my lap and also sleeps right next to me.

Walking in the dog park one day with my newly-adopted dog, I encountered quite a few women who also were first-time dog owners, having transferred their love of nurturing from children who didn't quite need it on a day-to-day basis to an animal.

The empty-nest years are as perfect a time as any to bring an animal companion into the house for empty nest single parents. My friend Arden Moore, an animal expert with whom I previously worked as a journalist with a south Florida newspaper, points out that animals are significantly beneficial to our well-being.

Indeed, the benefits of pet ownership are well-documented. Studies show that pets decrease stress levels and in so doing can reduce blood pressure, reduce anxiety and its physical manifestations, increase mood and help those with PTSD, increase one's physical activity, lower heart disease, expand one's social life (through walks and visits to dog parks), and promote a sense of responsibility in feeding and caring for them.

I may live alone. But with my animal companion in the house, I'm never lonely.

Consider filling your empty nest with a companion animal such as a cat or a dog. Rescuing an animal is a wonderful avenue for doing so. Getting pet insurance is a good way to ensure you can handle any health problems that may arise. If it is not feasible at this time to rescue an animal, consider fostering pets until they find a forever home or spending some time volunteering at the local animal shelter. Animals not only provide companionship in your own environment but open the door to an entire new world of other animal lovers, which can lead to more human friendships.

CHAPTER NINE

EMBRACING THE SINGLE LIFE

Single life: I've been OK with it. And I've been not OK with it.

Relationships: I've had them and not been OK in them. And I've been in relationships that are OK.

The bottom line: you don't need to be in a relationship to be whole. But when you find the right person, it can amplify your happiness.

It is said that when you are not actively seeking a relationship is when you come to find it.

There is a school of thought regarding break-ups that it's good to let at least a year go by before jumping back into the dating pool again.

I see the wisdom of that advice. Being alone for at least a year puts you through the cycle of weekends, holidays, and birthdays by yourself so you have the time and opportunity to truly experience healing. You understand that the steering wheel to your happiness is not in someone else's hands, but your own. You appreciate your own strengths to handle situations on your own.

But sometimes the heart overrules the head. And it may open the door to a situation that is worse than the marriage you left.

For the most part, I waited a year after my divorce. When I dated someone while my sons were young and at home, I made a commitment that I would not be committed to that person under the same roof – it was important to me that I had the space to give my attention to them and their needs – my desire for full companionship could be put on hold when I became an empty nester.

One must come to the realization that when you bring someone into your life, it's not just your life into which you are bringing them – you are bringing them into your children's lives and that of your extended family, friends and even pets. Choose well.

A few years after I became an empty nester and after breaking off a long-term post-divorce relationship that wasn't in my best interests, I decided that I would retreat to my comfort zone of being OK with being alone.

Life had other plans.

* * *

When I was a student at Roosevelt High School in Wyandotte, Michigan in the mid-1970s, Rick was the last boy I'd ever consider giving even a passing glance.

I was a bookish honors student, the editor of the high school newspaper, the editor of the yearbook, a member of the synchronized swimming team, chorale singer, and a member of a student travel club.

Rick was voted 'Super Freak' for the yearbook. A photo shows him wearing a black leather jacket, smoking 'something' in a pipe whereas I was a member of Students Opposed to Smoking.

Little did I know that Rick was dealing with the death of his father, followed by the death of his mother, before he had even crossed the stage to accept his high school diploma. He was catapulted into the responsibilities of adulthood far quicker than the average young person.

We went our separate ways – he, the boy who secretly longed for a relationship with me – and me, the nerdy girl who would never contemplate a relationship with a 'super freak'.

I went on to earn a Bachelor's degree in journalism with honors from Central Michigan University and then moved to Florida to pursue job opportunities. Rick married and divorced within two years and then joined the Navy. Upon his return, he worked in various blue-collar jobs.

Fast forward 40 years. I'd gotten word that my high school class reunion was coming up. A private Facebook group page was formed to keep in touch on details.

I had no intention of going. My oldest son was dealing with a kidney issue and it looked like he may have had to have one of his kidneys removed.

I didn't have disposable income for a trip to Michigan for something that while it would be fun was not in my budget. I still had another son in college.

And I had a fear of flying.

Nonetheless, it was fun connecting with everyone on Facebook. One of the people who reached out to me to connect as a friend was Rick. I accepted the friend request and didn't think too much more about it until a few days later when I posted something about my yoga practice and he commented: "I love yoga. I've been doing it since the 1970s. I remember you taking a picture of me doing yoga for the high school newspaper."

Boing! That was it! That was the moment that Rick finally had caught my attention. I thought any person who continued a yoga practice for 40 years as a means of grounding himself and keeping physically fit was worth some attention. I had just started a serious yoga practice myself and here was a man who'd been committed to it for four decades.

As the weeks passed, Rick and I chatted through Facebook Messenger. We shared details about our families and jobs. After I moved to Florida to work for a daily newspaper, I eventually became a freelance journalist and eventually a single mother of two, divorced after 15 years before entering my second long-term relationship that I ended after 12 years, which had been defined by a great deal of emotional abuse.

I wrote to him of how, in my 50s, I began engaging in many 'firsts': I got my first dog, joined the local U.S. Masters Swimmers, took up yoga and studied meditation.

He told me of his work with an air conditioning products manufacturing company. He was the father of one son, two stepsons and a step-daughter and a grandfather to five grandchildren.

He shared about how the death of his wife of 27 years was the most difficult experience of his life and how he had to keep going for his children and grandchildren.

Rick told me of how he grounded himself every morning in yoga and meditation and further took care of himself through working out in the gym and running. He told me he found it refreshing to correspond with someone who actually knew something about yoga and meditation.

Meanwhile, it was looking more like I wasn't going to attend our high school reunion and that my son would have surgery. Rick – a man I hadn't seen in 40 years – told me if there was anything he could do to let him know. He indicated that if I visited family at Christmas to look him up.

I told him he had already done so much for me by listening to me with compassion, that I was glad he reached out to request the Facebook connection and that life has a funny way of manifesting experiences for us. He concurred.

About a month after I began to correspond with Rick via Facebook came the good news: I was going to the reunion. My son's nephrologist opted to not remove his kidney, opening the door. The financial challenge was mitigated when one of my high school classmates had generously offered me some of her frequent flyer miles to help me offset the costs.

"I hope my yoga mat packs nicely into a suitcase because I'm coming to the reunion!" I wrote.

"That's great," he replied. "I look forward to seeing you." Although Rick promptly responded, his comments were typically brief.

I was hoping he'd invite me to do yoga with him. He didn't.

A few weeks before the reunion, I asked Rick about its location. Of course, it is the 21st century and anyone can find any address with GPS-enabled apps.

He gave me the address.

I thanked him and told him I'd have to ask my mother something I hadn't done since I was in high school: if I could borrow her car.

I was met with Internet silence. Then...

"LOL...if you need a ride let me know."

"I may take you up on that," I replied. (Are you kidding? Of course I wanted to go with him!)

When it came time for the reunion, I flew into Detroit, meditating the entire way and thus mitigating my fear of flying.

I had gotten into town and took in an art fair with my mother and sisters. My mother casually referred to Rick's offer to drive me to the reunion as a date and I rejected the notion: "No, it's not a date. It's a ride."

On the day of the reunion, Rick came to pick me up at my mother's house (my childhood home) from his own apartment just three blocks away. He complimented me on the way I had dressed and lamented that he hadn't dressed better, assuming that the reunion dress code was casual (it was, but I *wanted* to get dressed up!).

We went out to his car and he stood by me at the passenger's side, opening the door for me to get in. He took his seat and before he turned the keys in the ignition, turned to face me.

"I haven't been on a date for a very, very long time," he said to me. "I didn't know how to dress. I didn't know whether to bring you flowers."

"This *is* a date," I thought, then said aloud, "Rick, I haven't been in a relationship for a year and a half. Let's just go and have fun."

We got to the reunion and I felt like an alien – albeit a happy one – among people I haven't seen for 40 years. Save for the name tags, I wouldn't have been able to pick out any of them in a line-up. A photographer was on hand to capture photographs of us as we looked now to assemble for a yearbook. Clippings from the high school newspaper I used to edit were on display. A somber list of those who are now deceased was displayed on a poster.

I happily reminisced with people about our high school days.

Then Rick asked me to dance.

"I'm not a very good dancer," I said, but took him up on it, rationalizing that if I made a fool of myself, I'd be heading back to Florida within a few days.

We danced. And danced. And danced. I kicked my shoes off and danced some more. Rick danced with wild abandon.

Sometimes we sat out the dance and just belted out the song from our table in what amounted to a private karaoke performance.

Dinner was served, but we picked at it. Out of nervousness, neither one of us could hardly eat. Rick had been secretly shoving mints into his mouth.

The side glances started shooting our way: "Rick and Carol?"

Yes – what in high school would have been regarded as the most unlikely pairing was starting to fuse that night.

With a handful of other classmates, we closed the place down. Rick asked if I wanted to go somewhere else. My hometown isn't like the town in Florida in which I live where there are plenty of places to hang out 24/7. For a lack of places to go, I indicated we should just drive back to my mother's house.

As he walked me to the door, I reached out to take his hand. At the door, we hugged and gave each other a quick kiss.

What just happened? I went to my high school reunion and now...a romance?

It turns out that high school reunions are indeed an opportunity for creating new romance.

According to the website classmates.com, eight million people attend reunions each year and 57 percent are looking forward to reconnecting with former sweethearts or crushes. It can be infinitely preferable to online dating because the couple already knows so much about how the other person was raised, schooled and what kind of community shaped their journey into adulthood.

In a Psychology Today article on the topic, one couple -- she being a writer, he being a professional poker player -- decided they weren't going to let geography, fear and external criticism keep them from creating the relationship they want going into their older adult years.

One of my cousins is married to a man she met at her high school reunion. She's over-the-moon happy.

So, beyond dancing and singing with the guy I wouldn't give two minutes to back in high school, what is it about Rick that made me want to explore a relationship with him?

We were free to do so. He had been widowed for two and a half years and I was no longer in a committed relationship at that point. I made a pact with myself that I would not even as much go on one date until I cycled through an entire year of holidays and my birthdays without being involved with someone. I wanted to feel what it was like to be alone and make a relationship decision out of choice, not a fear of being alone.

He is kind and respectful. He is not threatened by the fact that I am a professional woman and a journalist at that. He is not possessive of my work time. He is aware of and understood why I did a background check on him.

Rick understands I have taken care of myself since I was 21years old and have been the sole or primary breadwinner for my family, both as a married woman and a single mother, so nobody is going to come into my life and start telling me what I can or can't do, a problem that had been part of a previous relationship.

He states his needs so that I am cognizant about what makes him happy and because of that open communication, I don't have to play guessing games. Communication is so important and we've been doing a lot of it as we create the foundation for the type of relationship we want.

He trusts me and that is so critical in a long-distance relationship.

He takes care of his body through exercise. While we can't help external circumstances that can alter the trajectory of our health, we can lessen the impact by staying healthy and fit so no one else has to take care of us because of poor mistakes we've made.

He meditates. His desire to go inside himself to create inner peace is very attractive and the results are very evident.

He loves his family. While I chose to end my relationships, it wasn't his choice that his wife died. Yet I can see how much he loved her and that meant he would also treat me with that same respect. He loves his children and grandchildren and spends a great deal of time with them.

He values people over monetary stuff. He loves animals and my dog took to him like he was one of her favorite treats. When your dog approves of your prospective partner, that's a good sign.

We share our emotions: we laugh like crazy and have cried together.

We have shared interests of yoga, exercise, meditation, music, and other interests.

That's just for starters.

Given that, we decided to go for it. Rick made flight arrangements to visit with me in south Florida a month after the reunion and we've been flying back and forth to see each other ever since.

One of his flights to Florida came at the time Hurricane Irma was about to hit. He spent three days with me in a pet-friendly Red Cross shelter, sleeping on the floor on sleeping bags with hundreds of other people as we ate school cafeteria food and couldn't shower for three days.

When we returned to my house and I had to get back to work, he spent his vacation week lifting a tree that fell onto my car, chain-sawing other trees that fell down and cleaning out my refrigerator and freezer as the power outage spoiled everything inside.

We 'see' each other in nightly video chats and talk with each other before we go to work and during our lunch breaks. We've created a playlist of songs on Spotify, with our shared love of music

Forty years ago, I wouldn't have given Rick a second thought.

Now, because of a class reunion, I can't stop thinking about him.

It had always been important to me that whoever was in my life as a partner had to be someone who got along well with my sons.

On the other hand, I also hoped that whomever my ex-husband partnered with would have a good relationship with my sons as well.

There are other dynamics for adult children of divorce, such as the choice of the parent with whom they will spend particular holidays. Eventually, as they pair up, their choices will expand to their partners' parents as well. Try to endeavor to make this decision as devoid of stress as possible for your offspring. If an approaching holiday means you'll be alone, make plans as soon as possible to ensure that the way you will spend the day will create joy in your life without guilt in your adult children's lives.

If and when you are ready to start dating, there is a lot of public information available on people that can offer a general sense of the person with whom you are contemplating a date. In addition to a generic Internet search – including social media sites – run their names through local, county, state and federal law enforcement databases. You can comb through criminal records as well as any civil lawsuits. Property ownership can be researched as well and inform you of whether someone is living with someone else. Marriage and divorce records also are good resources for establishing whether someone is being honest with you. Second and subsequent marriages have a higher failure rate, so the last thing you want to do when entering another relationship is go from the frying pan to the fire.

CHAPTER TEN

LEGACY – THE END IS THE BEGINNING

This book is about being a empty nester single parent. Essentially, though, that is a label and it is not who you truly are. Think about all of the 'labels' you take on throughout your life. Baby. Adolescent. Teen. Young Adult. Job Title. Marital status. Spouse. Parent. Grandparent.

The labels come and go. But the essence of who we are remains.

Some in society have unfairly labeled the single mother as lazy and lacking in moral fortitude when nothing could be further from the truth. Sometimes divorce IS in the best interest of the children. And we are among the hardest – if not the hardest – workers in the day-to-day existence of humanity. We singularly do what it takes two people to do. Our focus on our children is laser-sharp and contrary to what some believe, our children did not grow up running amok in the streets.

Some of the most successful men and women in our society grew up in a single-parent household. One even became the president of the United States.

And so, as we single parents enter our empty nest years, our life focuses on our legacy.

What will we leave behind?

We leave behind the values that we championed while raising our children alone.

Resiliency.

Courage.

Determination.

Hard work.

How to live on less and value people more than possessions.

The lesson that a home is more important than a house.

The lesson of not compromising one's values.

Finding joy in the simplest of things.

The importance of family.

Learning lessons from adversity.

How to honor your body, mind and spirit.

It's OK to be alone and it's equally wonderful to be part of a community.

I will end this book the way I started it with this quote:

"This could be our finest hour. To let go when we want to hold on requires utmost generosity and love. Only parents are capable of such painful greatness." - psychologist Dr. Haim Ginott

Let go. Have faith that you did the best you could. Sit back and watch how your labor has borne fruit. Your finest hour now is to show your children, the world at large – and even yourself – what it means to live a life of purpose at any age or stage of life.

Put together a blueprint for the life you want to build on the foundation you have thus far created. And start constructing it!

ABOUT THE AUTHOR

Writing – particularly journalism – has been in Carol's blood ever since she was in junior high school, where she served as the editor of the student newspaper. She went on to become the editor of her high school paper and yearbook. During her senior year of high school, Carol landed a job at her hometown weekly newspaper - *The Wyandotte News-Herald.* From then, Carol attended Central Michigan University, where she worked as a copy editor and a reporter on the student newspaper, *CM LIFE,* and executed an internship at the *Saginaw News* until she graduated with honors and a Bachelor's degree in journalism. Carol then took a job as a reporter at the now-defunct Scripps-Howard newspaper *The Hollywood Sun-Tattler* in Hollywood, Florida. After two years, she was hired at the *Fort Lauderdale News and Sun-Sentinel* (now called the *South Florida Sun-Sentinel*) where she covered politics, religion, human interest features and education. Carol won the Newsmaker Award from the Florida Teaching Profession/National Education Association for Distinguished News Coverage of Public Education in Florida. As a freelance writer, Carol has been honored in the Cassell Network of Writers/Florida Freelance Writers Association writing competitions. At the time of this writing, Carol holds membership in the Society of Professional Journalists, the Society of Environmental Journalists, the Society for Advancing Business Editing and Writing, Cassell Network of Writers, and the Florida Freelance Writers Association. She worked and raised her two sons from her home in south Florida. Learn more at www.writingservicespro.com. You also can connect with Carol at Brzozowski.carol@gmail.com, @brzozowski on Twitter and www.linkedin.com/in/carolbrzozowski/

Printed in Great Britain
by Amazon